MIGHT IN MOTION

MIGHT IN MOTION

Motivation Momentum
Mindfulness Might

MARIANNA L. KINNEE

MIGHT
IN
MOTION

Might In Motion, LLC

Contents

Maria and Eva – You are my inspiration daily to create a positive legacy. I love you both dearly!

Introduction

Might In Motion focusses on four key area of growth called the "Four M's": Motivation, Momentum, Mindfulness, and Might. This book will guide you in manifesting these four areas into your deserved life and career path. Together, we will identify and navigate your personal and professional goals to bring your journey to greater, more meaningful heights.

Let's define the Four M's:

- **Motivation** – Focus on your **why**.
- **Momentum** – Focus on **moving forward**.
- **Mindfulness** – Focus on your **mental well-being**.
- **Might** – Focus on your **physical health**.

All too often, we get so distracted and bogged down that we forget what our "big picture" looks like. By breaking down your focus into the Four M's, you will successfully create an action plan to progress in these areas, thus propelling you forward to achieve your goals.

The Might in Motion journey you are about to embark on will provide you with the necessary tools to push yourself outside your comfort zone. We will guide you every step of the way, including walking you through valuable hands-on challenges in each chapter.

When you begin new work in any area of life - weight loss,

finding a new job, learning a new skill - you can spend hours, days, weeks or months trying to find the optimal plan to achieve the end goal. By being so focused on trying to find the "fastest" or "best" way to accomplish these things, we never do them. What in your life have you been thinking of doing, but haven't? What is stopping you from starting? If you are looking for permission - here it is. Start today, even if it is just one small step. In order to get where you want to go, you have to leave where you are.

Take a moment before you begin reading to ask yourself: Are you going through the motions, or taking action?

Get ready, because it's time!

3 - 2 -1 - ACTION!

Notes

Motivation

I

Discover Your Why

Inside of you is the power to construct the life you yearn for, and your thoughts and actions will determine weather of not you succeed in manifesting it. It is your duty to take full accountability for your actions, behavior, and choices, and to make very conscious decisions about which paths you take. Before you can do any of this with intention, you must know your WHY.

Have you ever thought about your WHY? It is a question many of us are trained to stop asking when we are kids. Now is the time for you to start to ask it again.

In your first challenge, you will discover your WHY, by working backwards. You will start by identifying four goals you want to achieve. These can be goals focused on your career, relationships, physical or mental well-being, or another area of your life that is important to you. As you define your goals, rate yourself on whether or not you are truly ready to put in the effort to achieve them. Use a scale from 1 (low – not willing to put in the effort) to 10 (high – you are READY and WILLING to put in the effort). Be honest with yourself in your ratings. If the goals you want to achieve are those you know will bring you closer to your ideal life, but you are not willing to put in the effort, your WHY is not strong enough. And that is OK, because discovering it is what this chapter is all about.

CHALLENGE:

Visualize your ideal life. What does it look like? What must you do to achieve it? Write down four goals you want to focus on that will bring you closer to where you want to be. Carry them with you. Post them where you can see them. Read them every day. As you do, ask yourself; WHY do I want to achieve these things? WHY do these goals matter to me? WHY haven't I taken action on them yet? As you begin to ask yourself these questions, your actual Why will reveal itself. And once you know your Why, you will become unstoppable, and gain a newfound sense of motivation.

Having Trouble Identifying Your Goals & Your Why's? First, don't overthink this. Pay attention to what popped into your mind first. Second, here are some prompts if you need help getting started: Would you like to be in better shape? Have a healthier mindset? Have stronger, more meaningful relationships? Make more money? Help more people? Leave a more robust legacy? Build a business? Learn a new skill? Become better at public speaking? Once you have your Goals written down, then focus on your Why for each (or for all, as it could be the same).

Example Goal #1: Become better at public speaking.

Example Why: Once I'm more comfortable speaking in front of an audience, it will help me grow my business, and provide for my family at a greater level. (In this example, the "Why" is Family).

Notes

2

Saying Yes vs. No & Defining Your Mission

In order to achieve your goals, you need to start saying NO to things. There is no way around this fact. Reaching greater, more fulfilling levels in life takes work, and you will need to reallocate your time to focus on this work. If you have always been known as the one that "gets things done" or "is always there to help out", then saying "no" may prove difficult for you to do, and feel foreign. So, as an added layer to your Goals & Why defined in Chapter 1, it's now time to define your Mission, which will help keep you even more focused on the work you must do. Your mission becomes the guide path that you can follow with confidence.

Your mission should summarize your values. It is typically a short statement and easy to memorize. For example, mine is "I build positive legacies." By having a clear statement of your personal mission, you can begin to filter out the noise of all the clutter in your life. Write your mission down every day. When things pop up, think about if that new shiny thing fits into your mission. If it doesn't then respectfully decline it.

The goals that you defined in the prior chapter, should align with your mission. This can take several forms. For example, I set goals each year that will help me to maintain my physical fitness. This allows me to "build positive legacies" with those around me that may need that example to live a healthier lifestyle. After seeing me drink a gallon of water a day for a year, my husband suddenly began to do the same. My actions to take care of myself, allowed another person to be inspired.

Another goal that I have is to help others at work grow and build their carriers. This too follows my mission. For example, I was asked by my leader to present to a group about a project I had handed off 6 months prior to another team. After some questions back and forth via chat, I said "Let's talk about this next week in my one-on-one." I didn't just say "yes" because I knew it doesn't fit into my goals and would take away the opportunity for the new team to own the project. This gives me time and space to respectfully divert the request to the right group. In the past, I would have just said yes right away and taken on the increased workload. This would not have benefited me and would have been counter to my mission.

Saying no right now does not mean no forever. So, make your YES count. Say YES to what matches your mission and moves your goals forward. That is be beautiful thing about having a personal mission that can guide your direction.

CHALLENGE:

Over the next seven days reflect on any items you said yes or no to. Why did you make that choice? Did your decisions help you move toward your goals? As you become more aware of your decisions, you will find that you will make decisions that are more aligned with what is important to you.

Notes

3

Money, Money, Money

Historically, have you believed money is the root of all evil? What if I told you money is not inherently bad, and that making money is actually the right thing to do?

When you make money, you are able to help more people than if you didn't. For instance, if you have limited funds but wanted to help your local community, you could volunteer a limited amount of your time working at the local shelter or food bank. But if you had instead created wealth for yourself, you could have been in a position to actually build those shelters or food banks, and not only help those in need of such facilities, but also offer employment opportunities to those in your community.

If after giving this concept some thought, you are in agreement money is NOT the root of all evil, and that you can do good in the world when you have it, then you are morally obligated to go and get it. So how do you do that?

Reflect on your goals. Every day do things that will move you in the direction of building wealth to fund your giving back dreams

Understand your worth. Research the marketplace so that you understand what value your time and effort really are worth and then go above and beyond in adding so much value that they can't deny you a raise.

Identify additional income streams. This could be with new businesses or real estate ventures. There are so many ways you can bring in additional income. For example, I have taught my two girls how selling their old toys will generate income. My youngest (6 at the time) sold all her Mini Mouse items (that she hadn't touched in a year) in 2 days for over $50. She was so excited and was able to turn that income into Christmas presents for others.

When there is uncertainty, you can be tempted to chase the money. This could mean forgetting the need to come from a place of service. When you come from a place of service, then money will be a byproduct of your success. Building that trust through helping other people will drive credibility in your field of expertise. That is the long game. Focus on the vision of the impact you will have on others. It will take time, but your success will come. Your vision will be fulfilled and then the money will come with it.

CHALLENGE:

Review your income streams and evaluate how approaching your business from a place of service to others could actually lead to increased wealth. Reflect and journal on this over the next week and then contemplate how your point of view on the topic may have shifted.

Notes

4

Fear

What are you afraid of?

Fear is one of the greatest of all motivators. When the fear of not doing something becomes larger than the fear of doing that thing, you are on the cusp of great change! And more times than not, we must to do the things that frighten us in order to level-up.

Think about what may be holding you back at work. Are you afraid to go after that next promotion? Are you afraid to take on that big project? Are you afraid to present your ideas to the VPs? Really reflect on the why. Is it more responsibility? Is the risk of not getting the job? Is it potential embarrassment? I always ask this question when a mentee comes to me with a fear: "What is the worst thing that could happen?" If that worst case is really no big deal, then suck it up, buttercup, and go do the thing that frightens you the most. You may be surprised how quickly that fear will turn to dust when you take that risk!

Think about your health goals. Are you afraid of finally losing the weight because that was your crutch to hide you from the world?

For me, I became so afraid that my health would prevent me from having the active lifestyle I wanted to share with my daughters, that I finally took action. My goal started out small at first (walking my neighborhood) that soon transitioned to losing 50 pounds, which then transitioned to running 5Ks, 10Ks, and even a half marathon!

Facing your fears may seem unconnected to being motivated to achieve your goals. Many times, on your journey to reaching your goals, you will be faced with forks in the road. These become your greatest opportunities to really stretch outside your comfort zone and "expand to expand." In order to stay on the path toward your vision, you need to look at the opportunity in front of you and ask the following questions: "Will this move me toward my goals? What does conquering this fear do to help me overcome other fears?"

CHALLENGE:

As you reflect on your four goals, journal about the fear that is motivating you to achieve these goals. Identify one big fear that you have, and then execute putting yourself in that fear. Is it snakes? Go to the pet store and hold one. Is it telling someone you care about them? Pick up the phone or pen and paper and tell them. Is if being raw and honest with your partner about your relationship fears? Tell them. DO NOT WAIT. Do it today. Execute it today. This will help you to see that you can overcome your biggest fears and therefore you can overcome the fears that may be holding you back from your goals!

Notes

5

Choose Your Hard

The saying "Choose your hard or the hard will choose you" is a powerful one, and proactively choosing your hard is empowering. Here's an example: At work, if you're often asked to help with various efforts outside of your normal job description, be proactive in throwing your name in the ring for tasks you know will expand your skillset vs. getting selected for ones that won't. Or, if you have a relationship in your life that needs mending, be the first to reach out, and actively work to repair it. By being in control as much as possible, when the unexpected hard times do arrive at your doorstep, you'll be better prepared to handle them. They will also very likely come to you less & less, as once you assume a position of full control, it's remarkable how other areas of your life begin to improve, become less chaotic, more predicable, and more fulfilling.

Fun Fact: Did you know the human brain loves challenges? However, only if they're within a specific range of difficulty. You experience peak motivation when you are at the edge of your current abilities. This is the called the Goldilocks Rule. You don't want things to be too hard or too easy; when they are "just right" your motivation will flourish. This also leads to an improved level of self-confidence.

As you begin to develop a steady stride toward reaching your goals, it will be critical to begin challenging yourself in new ways — big and small. Start trying new ways to do things, and add new challenges where they seem fitting. This will allow you to expand, and drive your levels of motivation to new levels.

CHALLENGE:

Review your four goals and the progress you are making (or not making) toward achieving them. Is something proving to be harder than you thought? How can you overcome that? Document the challenges you are facing, and create a plan to overcome them by choosing to do the hard work, before the hard work chooses you, and becomes a true roadblock in your journey to reaching the next level.

Notes

6

Team Motivation

Do you lead a team? As a leader, you have an opportunity to help your team set goals that will help you on your journey. When you have energy around team goals, the whole team can feel the power! For example, when you are talking about your goals, are you speaking in a dull, monotone voice? Or are you animated and excited? When you naturally have excitement, then others know that your goals are attractive. It will pull others to align with your vision and they in turn will be more inclined to support your goals and team productivity will naturally go up.

It is important to figure out what types of motivation triggers the highest outcome in your ability to deliver. This is important to understand, especially in the workforce. You can use that knowledge to ensure you are staying engaged in the goals your leader has set for you and how your team engages in yours. It is also important to understand how your employees are motivated. By leveraging that knowledge, you will be able to rally them to do even more. Here are different types of motivation and their meanings:

- Intrinsic - driven to accomplish a task because you find it personally rewarding
- Competence / Learning - an individual's need to feel competent or capable
- Attitude - drives you to change the way you or other people think and feel
- Creative - motivated by the desire to express yourself in an artistic / creative way
- Extrinsic - promise of a reward or a threat of punishment
- Achievement - satisfaction gained when reaching a goal and being recognized publicly
- Affiliation - desire to belong to a certain group of people or an organization
- Incentive - earning predetermined compensation for above-average performance

If you are a new (or experienced) manager, motivating your team can be daunting. You want to create an environment of vitality and fulfillment. Doing that not only grows company culture but also personal fulfillment for your team. Set team and individual goals for each associate by leveraging the types of motivation above. Clearly define the why and purpose of your team. Structure the team and roles so that they offer optimal levels of challenge, control, variety, and collaboration for the individual.

Inspiration. This is what separates bosses from great leaders. Do you want to be a leader? Your actions will be what motivates others. You use your actions to inspire others to dream more, learn more, do more and become more. Great leaders will put their teams first. That means that the teams needs are met first. It means that you may have to sacrifice in order to protect and serve others. We all know people that are true inspirational leaders. They may be the lowest rank, yet they can move armies of people to do great things.

To be a motivational change-maker, you realize that you cannot go it alone. You must seek out diverse perspectives. Seek this from unexpected places and people. You don't always need the most "powerful" person to help with the solution. You need to work with the front-line team to understand the real opportunities. By hearing them, you will be able to motivate and stride toward solutions that really change the operation you are working to improve. Stay positive and surround yourself with creative and supportive people. Who you surround yourself will influence you a great deal. Those that are in your inner circle have a tremendous impact on you and your team's ability to accomplish those goals that you have set out to achieve.

CHALLENGE:

Evaluate your team goals. Are they inspirational and attractive? How is each of your associates motivated based on the list above? What can you do over the next 30 days to connect with them in their motivational language? Take these learnings and execute some changes. Journal on how those changes impact you and the trajectory of the team.

Notes

Momentum

7

Connection With Your Vision

Old school TV's had antennas. You had to point them in the direction of the station you wanted to watch. Is your antenna tuned to the direction you want to go? If not, there is a disconnect between where you are now and where you want to be, and that will no doubt impact the quality and speed of your progress, and your overall forward momentum.

Momentum requires you to make steady progress in your goals. As you focus your attention on the actions you are taking, make sure those actions are pointing you in the direction you want to go in. If you need to "reset" your compass, it may mean taking a time-out, and auditing where you're at, including your Goals.

Try this: Write your four goals down again, but this time, as if they already happened (and if any new Goals have popped into your mind since, add those to your list). For example, if one of your goals is to pay off your car, then write "My car is paid in full and I have my car papers in my hand." Or if you have a goal to increase your family net worth, then write "My family's net worth is X and this money is accessible in our accounts.". The idea here is to really feel what it would be like to have already accomplished your goals. Let that feeling continue to drive you forward, and help keep you on course.

Reminder: Physically writing down your goals every day (or as often as you need to) and taking daily action on them will condition your mind and body to believe they have already occurred. When you believe those goals are already real at a cellular level, the universe will speed up their reality. Now that you have begun to connect with your vision at a cellular level, imagine the board of directors who are in your mind running your life. Name these characters - bring them to life! In your journal you can even draw them. What are they all doing and saying when you are faced with a difficult decision? Just like the movie Inside Out, they all are different. Some are full of positivity and others doubt. Some will find creative solutions and others want to stay on the known path. As you work to drive progress toward your vision, difficult situations will come up. Take time to reflect on what each of these directors in your mind would do. Which of them are holding back your progress and why? Use that insight to take steps based on who you want to guide you. You can use that knowledge to your advantage in those moments.

CHALLENGE:

By this Chapter, your goals should be well defined. But if you're having trouble connecting with them and making progress, begin to write them down daily, and write them down as if they have already happened. Add new goals to your list. Don't be afraid to add BIG goals to your list as well, thinking far out into the future. For added help, break your goals down into smaller steps (3-5 per goal) specific to the actions you can take in the next 30 days. At the end of the 30 days, reevaluate your progress.

Notes

8

Connection With Others

When you move throughout the world, you have to push against something. Until 2022, physics thought this to be a law- the law of conservation of momentum. Researchers from Georgia Tech proved the opposite. When bodies exist in curved spaces, they can move without pushing against something. Where in your life are you maintaining momentum by pushing off of something (or someone) in a negative way? This is your opportunity to shift your approach to a curved mindset. Where can you create your own motion? How much more of a positive impact will you have on those around you by removing negativity? This is your chance to make that shift and create momentum in a creative and positive way.

Momentum starts and ends with you. But while you are on your journey to reaching your vision, you will need others. You have to take those first steps to connect with others and build out your network in a positive way where both parties find value. A network will allow you to discover hidden treasures about yourself and uncover opportunities for you to give back and help others. Building that network can be a challenge, especially when you may be working from home or are starting a new business.

Social media is another resource that can be used in so many ways. You can explore new recipes to try, get inspired for a future wedding day or learn the latest dance craze. Did you know you can also leverage it to propel your career? This isn't just for the entrepreneurs anymore. By leveraging platforms like LinkedIn, you can create a professional presence. You can follow companies and leaders you admire on many platforms. This is very helpful if you are interviewing for a role in a new company. By doing research via different avenues, the questions you ask your interviewer may change and could help you stand out from the crowd. There are so many groups in LinkedIn to follow and be active in that you can grow your knowledge of any industry exponentially by participating in a resource that is readily available to you.

Carve out time on your calendar to purposefully reach out to others that you may not connect with on a regular basis. Set up meet and greets or call them to chat and catch up. Those connections build longer term relationships that are beneficial to both you and them. Just like dating, you have to be intentional with this action. When you are intentional in creating these connections, you are able to foster relationships where both parties can gain something. This may be insight into a problem needing solution, realizing you can connect them to someone else in your network, supporting growth in others - creating ripples of positive shifts.

CHALLENGE:

Over the next 30 days, connect with 4 new people each week. You will quickly see how saying YES to momentum will uncover amazing opportunities. In addition, post or comment daily (if only for five to ten minutes a day) on professional networking sites, like

LinkedIn. The increase in activity will move you up in what people see in their feeds. That will place you top of mind for recruiters, or others you are looking to attract into your space.

Notes

9

Service To Others

Staying focused on your goal can be hard. Have the mindset of the servant in the Bible who keeps the lamp burning awaiting the return of the Master. You never know when your successes are coming. You can only remain focused on being at the ready and preparing for their arrival.

How do you prepare for the arrival of your success? First - be dressed for success. It seems so simple, but getting out of your comfy clothes and into professional dress can actually shift your energy. Even if you are working from home, make sure you are dressing for success. Second - live in service mode. When you are giving and providing service to others you will shine brighter. By adding value, you will be seen as the go to person and that will open opportunities to you. Third - remain in action. Each day ensure you have items that you will do that will move you toward your big goal.

Momentum requires resiliency, not happiness. Having a positive outlook and experiencing happiness is very different from "being happy." When you layer a positive outlook on events that happen, you open yourself to more positive events. You can never "be happy" all the time but approaching life with resiliency and positivity helps you to remain motivated to achieve the goals you have set for yourself. Serving others is a great way to foster resiliency and positivity – a combination for success.

CHALLENGE

As you go through your day, look for the opportunities to show resiliency and positivity. When you reach the end of your day you will reflect back and see the wins as a glorious collection of moments that you can bank to maintain your momentum. Over the next 30 days, as you journal about your day, note moments where you showed resiliency or service. Find joy in those moments.

Notes

10

Connection With Yourself

I'm a big fan of celebrations! When I set out my plans to reach a goal, I like to have micro victories along the way that I can celebrate. For example, when I hit a weight loss milestone target on my way to my larger, long-term goal, I treated myself to a spa day. When I got a promotion, I had been going for, I treated myself to a new pair of shoes. Sometimes my reward may be as simple as carving out time for a hot bath. Other times, more extravagant. Before you celebrate you need to ensure you are doing these 3 steps:

1. Get in the game. No one will notice you if you are not actively participating. This means adding value and solving problems.
2. Play the game. You have to learn the skills needed to succeed. This is crucially important in the speed we all live in today. Work with those that you know you can learn from and be a sponge.
3. Win the game. I love the concept that every day there is an opportunity to win or lose the day. When you rack up

daily wins, then you win the month and so forth. Set specific actions on a daily basis that will allow you to reach your long-term goals. Track your wins and losses. Soon you will find that you are on track to reach the goals you have set out to achieve.

If you don't celebrate you, who will? By setting out micro victories for following these three steps, you will be able to remain positive as you achieve your goals. All those victories begin to stack up. Winning attracts winning. As you reflect on your big goals, break them down into 30 / 60 / 90-day targets with rewards along the way. You will soon find that those rewards will encourage you to do more than you thought at a quicker pace!

CHALLENGE:

It can prove difficult at times to maintain momentum; we can become easily drained of energy for various reasons, even when following our passion. Every 30 days, audit the month prior (e.g., the first week of July, audit the month of June). Make an honest assessment of your progress, wins, and losses. Use that assessment to adjust your approach. This will be time well spent, and help ensure you are progressing towards your goals in a manner that aligns with your Mission. You may need to adjust communication with your team, change your operational strategy, or add more value to your customers. Just like with your phone, Reset, Recharge, and Recalibrate. It will ensure you are operating at your highest possible level!

Notes

11

Rituals

What rituals do you have? When you are getting ready for a date you may shave or get your hair done. All is done in preparation for a big, exciting event. The same mentality can be applied to maintaining momentum toward your goals. To create a ritual, you practice associating a habit with something you enjoy. For example, if you are on the way to the beach, you may play happy upbeat music. The next time you are feeling down, playing that music will bring back those positive feels of a fun beach trip.

You can find similar habits that will keep you motivated on your goals. If you have a fitness goal, then playing "Eye Of The Tiger" on the way to the gym may amp you up for a great workout. If you are working on a critical presentation for work, putting on your headphones with no sound on may help you remain focused on the task by drowning out the rest of the world.

Rituals are not all about sound (or lack thereof). I set out my clothes the night before every single day. I also make my bed (even if it is just my side if my husband is still asleep) when I get up. These are rituals I started when I was very young. It allows me to start my day ahead of the game. Ready to achieve what is ahead of me. I liken it to a knight approaching his armor. It is set out with a plan and a purpose. Even while working from home, I make sure I'm up and out of my PJ's to start the day.

Another helpful ritual, is to work in surges. When you work in surges you can really ride the wave of momentum. I like to work on goals in 3-month increments. Within that 3 months you focus completely on the sub-goals you want to achieve that will drive to the bigger goals. At the end of that period, you take a week to reflect on what you have built, what you could adjust in the future and then plan for the next wave. I actually purchase and use planners that are in 3-month sections to visually execute the ritual of working in surges. The act of physically writing down what and when I need to do things helps me to align my entire being on what I will accomplish in that time frame. These surges allow you to create consistent waves of momentum and keep you excited about your goals and how to get there.

CHALLENGE:

Spend one morning or evening this week (whichever proves to be the quieter or the two, so you can give yourself an uninterrupted block of time) document your 3-month targets. Take those and segment them into weekly actions. Create a ritual around this reflection time. This will create a habit that you will begin to repeat. You should do this every 3 months.

Notes

12

F.O.C.U.S.

Momentum is a mindset. What impact or end result are you moving towards? As you envision of how the puzzle comes together, you will see yourself move faster and faster to the end goal. This can be applied to any goal - weight loss, writing a book, starting a podcast, etc. When you are clear on the goal and how that goal will have a positive impact on others, you will find focus. All elements of the universe will begin to conspire to move you toward that clear vision. Your role is to take action every day toward that goal.

Lack of focus can drain you of your momentum and progress. Many of us have a hard time staying focused on one thing at a time. With so many distractions, I can relate to this - media, kids, phone, email, etc. If you talk to successful CEOs, they will tell you that multi-tasking will drain you and prevent you from achieving your goals. If you find that you are on the destructive path of distraction,

Curtis Tyrone Jones said, "Just because you're puzzled, doesn't mean life's jagged edges won't still fall into place for you." Are you remaining focused on your goals? As simple as the word FOCUS is, it really can make or break your momentum.

F - Forget Distractions - Anything that isn't going to help you achieve your mission should be removed.

O - Operate with Positivity - Your ability to stay positive in the face of adversity will help you maintain your vision.

C - Consistently Execute - Every day take steps toward your goal. No matter how small, those small steps will add up.

U - Unify to One Mission - As you unify around your mission, it will become easier to identify what will help you move forward.

S - Substance - Tangible results will come from the actions you take to remain on the path toward your goals.

I'd recommend you think about what is most important right now. Put all your energy into that thing. If you block off time in your day to read reports, work out, write that key presentation, you will find that you can achieve more and do it better. I literally turn my back to my computer or turn off notifications so that I can remain aligned with the item that I need to focus on right now.

CHALLENGE:

Get out that handy journal and write down all the things that distract you. Include things that are hurdles or roadblocks in your path to achieve your goals. Now that you have that list, you can see what your major disrupters are. Now write down how you are going to replace or change your distractions. This could be deleting that game from your phone that drains hours from your day, turning off email notifications so you can be present in a one-on-one, carving out time where it is just you and a loved one without any technology to suck you in.

Notes

Mindfulness

13

State Of Mind

What do you do every day to focus your mind? Your mind is the source of more power than you can imagine. When you focus on your goals and take time to meditate on them, you have the opportunity to manifest your outcomes. By visualizing having the success you desire, your mind begins to believe you have already achieved your goals. Once it believes it, opportunities to bring those goals to life will reveal themselves to you.

I recommend the book "Breaking the Habit of Being Yourself: How to Lose Your Mind and Create a New One" by Joe Dispenza. If you immerse yourself in the meditations, you will see and feel seismic shifts in your thinking and reacting to situations. For me, doing the practices in the book over 30 days was life changing. It helped me to break free from so much negative self-talk.

When your mind is unfocussed you open the door to all kinds of negative things. This could be temptations of the flesh; negative self-talk that takes you down a spiral of self-doubt or clouded vision. As this happens, you will see your thoughts deteriorate. You then will be confused on decisions and feel directionless. The best way to combat this is to refocus your mind. You can do this through prayer, meditation or visualization. 15 minutes spent without other distractions and focused on your choice of enlightenment will open up your mind and your path will be illuminated. Where you once felt like a boat without a rudder you will be clearer in your vision.

Mindfulness means taking time to be with yourself in creative ways. Invite yourself to coffee and have a chat with yourself. Pick up your favorite beverage and go hang out at a quiet spot. Keep your devices tucked away. Pull out your notebook and jot down things you notice about yourself in these quiet moments. As you find yourself letting your mind wander to your "to-do" list, refocus and ask yourself, "Is this going the way I want it to go?"

No one expects you to be Wonder Woman. We often expect that of ourselves. By taking moments to be alone and in tune with our thoughts and emotions, we are creating space for our own growth. That space will allow you to expand and have more to offer the world. You may be surprised what internal gems you discover.

CHALLENGE

Devote 15 minutes per day to meditation or visualization for the next 14 days. Those 15 minutes a day will allow you to be centered and you will begin to feel the shift within.

Notes

14

Give, Give, Give

Giving is life changing! Have you ever been in a bad mood when you are in the process of giving without expectation? I'd guess not. When you give, it isn't just the thing or the money or the time that you are offering up. You are also sending out positive energy. That positivity will shift you as well. The ripples of positivity will reach much further than just your immediate circle. It will expand beyond what you can see and impact others in a positive way. This act of living with kindness is simple, free and improves your mental health. It is good for your physical body (decreases blood pressure, stress levels) and your mind (boosts serotonin and dopamine).

Being mindful at work is just as important as being mindful when you are with your friends and family. So, what does mindfulness really mean? It means to be consciously present and tune in. This can be harder in a virtual world where multi-tasking is everywhere. When you are present you are aware of two parts of your experience. The first is what is going on around you. The second is what is going on inside of you. This allows you to manage your mental and emotional state. By managing those internal forces, you become more skilled at managing those external forces and changes. How does this help you give? For example, by being focused on the report you are creating, and becoming aware when your mind begins to wander, you will find that you can complete the task quicker. When you are having meetings or one on ones, do the same thing. Notice when you begin to multi-task or your eyes wander to your phone. Refocus on the people you are with. That will mean so much to them, it will reduce the need for redundant questions and help you to give your full self to those around you. Carve out time in your day to let your mind wander. That way you can remain more focused on what you need to be doing.

CHALLENGE

Incorporate one random act of kindness into your day, every day. Show love and service, without any expectations. Just do it for others. Journal daily on how making this shift without expectations has impacted your perspective, and whether you began to notice a difference in how others treated you. No expectations. Just bring your best and do your best to show others kindness, love and service.

Notes

15

Declutter Your Mind

Do you look at a pile of clothes and groan "I have to fold laundry"? Or do you have the mindset that says, "I get to fold laundry"? That little shift makes all the difference. When you look at a task with a "have to" attitude it seems like a worthless chore. Your whole being, down to the cellular level, comes together with dread. That makes your whole being sag. When you flip that little phrase to "get to", your energy shifts. You feel the purpose. You have more drive to do things right and end up with a more organized and less cluttered mind.

Are you ever bored? Really bored. No distractions. Is your mind so cluttered that you can't break free from the never-ending chaos? Being mindful may mean turning away from your laptop, phone or tablet. Be still and as your mind moves, leverage that as an opportunity to just write and have your thoughts flow. Becoming at ease with yourself and your thoughts will actually lead to more confidence in your own skin. Everyone around you will begin to notice that confidence shift.

We rarely are without distractions. Instant gratification and distraction are always in the palm of our hands. Stopping the distractions will challenge you to be mindful of your inner thoughts, needs and wants. It gives you the opportunity to feel, observe and experience reality and the world around you. When you take time to remove all of the stimuli it creates space in your mind for thoughts, ideas and peace.

As you practice this daily, you will begin to reap massive rewards. These include, but aren't limited to, new ideas, awareness of your body and solutions to problems. By helping us become more in tune with the present, mindfulness improves our wellbeing and increases overall contentment in life.

CHALLENGE

Dedicate 10 minutes a day to do NOTHING. Be bored. Sit in the silence. Journal about what you learn in those moments of mental solitude. Be selfish in those moments so that you can really hear what your body, mind and spirit need to stay energized and on target. Close this time with yourself by repeating an affirmation or prayer. Change the story you tell yourself into something powerful and positive. It will adjust your trajectory and help you move the direction you want.

Notes

16

Whine Or Wine

Have you ever made wine? It is exciting to do. You pick the grapes. You crush the grapes. You add water, enzymes, tannins and acid. It ferments. You bottle it. You open it the next day and it doesn't have the depth that you had wanted you may be shocked and tempted to throw it out. DON'T! Good things need to rest. Wine must rest. It matures. Everything comes together when you take the time to let the parts work together. This is the same with your goals. Stay focused. Stay patient. Give yourself (and others) grace. That little extra time will bring you to your dreams.

Do you ever feel like you are in a rut? Do you find your energy lacking and your forward momentum halted? We all hit roadblocks. When that happens, it helps to get away from the situation. I do this with my daughters when they get stuck with homework and start to get unraveled. I encourage them to go outside and run it out. Do something COMPLETELY different than the problem at hand. When you take 10 minutes to pull yourself out of the situation you will find that you are now able to focus and see things differently.

Be aware when you are becoming unraveled, pause and get out of your own way. You will then find a way out of your rut and around your roadblock. Think of mindfulness as cybersecurity for your wellbeing.

1. Question the basics - What are the things that are getting you off track? How did they get there? Who planted those seeds of doubt?
2. Question the user - What are you doing that are contributing to your goals? Are you giving it your all to stay committed to your mission?
3. Understand the risk - What happens if you stray off your desired course? What is the worst-case scenario if success doesn't happen?
4. Tell management to start over - Do you need to get back to the basics? How quickly can you adjust to get back on track?

When you are mindful of your actions and their impact, then you protect your mindfulness. Be aware and tack action to remain on course.

CHALLENGE:

Review the questions above and journal about them. Really reflect on each one (perhaps devote a week per question). Spend time on it over and over until you believe you and your root cause. Now you can address the root cause and get back on track.

Notes

Might

17

Let's Get Physical

How do you find power in your day-to-day life? Might can take many forms. As you build physical strength, your mental strength will follow. You begin to see that you can do more than you ever thought possible. Those small moves each day to hold yourself accountable in your physical realm will open your mind to overcome obstacles in your work and personal life.

If you want to get stronger mentally then you need to get stronger physically! Moving your body will help you move your mind. Going for a walk is an amazing way to start a fitness journey or add to what you currently do. Getting your steps in outside is even better. The air and sun help to clear your mind and spirit. I try to walk at least 30 minutes every day. I can hear you now - "who has the time for that?" You do! While walking, you can make phone calls, listen to conference calls, or even learn something from an audio book or podcast. Those steps add up and will help you to improve your overall health. If you want to be powerful in business, it starts with taking that first step!

Whatever motivates you - yoga, dance, running, boxing, swimming, hiking - do it! Get moving today. Exercise improves your mood and physical well-being. It lowers stress and can give you the opportunity to connect with other like-minded individuals. That community will push you to get better and stay consistent.

There are so many apps that you can have any kind of trainer you want right in your hand. I've used RockMyRun, Garmin Connect, and Nike Training Club. There are also other apps like Aaptive and AllTrails that are worth checking out. These apps allow you to work out whenever, wherever and however you are inspired each day

In 2021, I participated in a push up challenge. We picked a random partner and encouraged each other to increase the number of full push-ups we could do in 2 minutes. We were given 30 days. That challenge helped me to improve physically and mentally. It also had me face a fear – asking a random person I've never met to be my virtual partner. Even though we were in different parts of the country we encouraged each other daily. That accountability allowed us to improve exponentially. It also led to a powerful friendship where we continue to hold each other accountable in different areas of our life.

CHALLENGE

Find a partner and do this challenge together. It will not only build you up physically, but also it will open the door to a relationship that will make a positive impact in both your lives. Over the next 30 days, track the number of pushups you can both do in 2 minutes. Text each other daily on how many you have done. Cheer each other on!

Notes

18

The Blues

Many people are impacted by changes in the seasons. As cold weather begins to creep in, you may feel a bit of the winter blues. You can start to create habits now that will serve you all winter (and for the whole year). You can't change the weather and perhaps your favorite outside activity is harder to do. Here are some tips to continue to focus on your physical well-being during these darker months.

Keep up your sleep routine. Sleep is a HUGE part of mood. To improve sleep, go to bed and wake up at the same time every day. That routine will help train your body to rest. As soon as you wake up, expose yourself to light. These simple behaviors will boost your mood and energy.

Boost your mood with the right food. Considering the food you eat is important. Consuming protein with breakfast, lunch and dinner can enhance mood and prevent sugar and carb cravings later in the day. Foods high in vitamin D can also help balance your mood.

Do some physical activity. Even though being outside in the cold may not be ideal, there are other ways to get physical activity in. You can do yoga or strength training indoors. You can also adjust your schedule to get an outside workout during the day when it is the warmest.

Winter blues can take its toll, however the habits you form will set you up to be in a better place throughout the year. Start doing these small things now and you will be grateful later as they will create habits that you can leverage all year long!

CHALLENGE:

For 2 weeks, set and keep a bed and wake up time. Journal about how you feel at the end of the 2 weeks. Adjust those times as needed and then repeat for two more weeks. Do this repeated cycle for 2 months. At the end, reflect on how thoughtful adjustments in your sleep routine has impacted your mental and physical wellbeing.

Notes

19

Spirit Lifting

Do you move heavy things? There is more power in you that you may have thought. Lifting weights is an amazing thing to start adding to your physical plan. Your MIGHT plan means you WILL get stronger. Evaluate your workouts and if resistance or weight training aren't part of that, start adding that into your plan. Just like you can feel the win crossing a finish line, you will also feel that win doing a squat with more weight than you ever had. Looking in the mirror you can channel your inner warrior. That fighter will help you in all other aspects of your life.

Your heart is the most important muscle in your body. They are the center of everything and allow us to live full lives. It is so important to ensure we take time to improve its health so that it will be pumping goodness for a long time. You can't have your heart lift a dumbbell. To work it and help it get strong, you need to get it pumping. We have talked in this book how important it is to set goals. For example, if you are just beginning, then a good starting goal is at least 150 minutes of brisk activity a week, but if you don't want to sweat the numbers, just move more! Find forms of exercise you like and will stick with and build more opportunities to be active into your routine.

The hard part is the mindset portion. When we begin a fitness journey, that may mean time away from friends at happy hour or sitting for hours watching movies. It is tempting to let that pull down our spirit or tug at our heart. Yet there is an opportunity to not let that happen but to shift your togetherness time to something new. An idea is to maintain a social calendar that is tied to healthy activities. That way you are value stacking your time - improving relationships and your health. Go on walks and do your gab sessions while you move instead of sipping chardonnay. Ride bikes with your kids and see the joy of making memories on their faces. There are so many opportunities to value stack your time – just look for and create them.

CHALLENGE:

Over the next 30 days, invite a friend or family member to join you for a physical activity (i.e. go for a hike, do a dance class, etc.) each week. You may be pleasantly surprised on how these moments help your relationships.

Notes

20

Stretch And Rest

You are coming to the end of the Might In Motion journey. You have stretched your mindset. Now you need to physically stretch. We have all seen a million 30-day challenges. My favorites by far are those that force me to slow down. Stretching is a great way to slow down and ensure you are caring for your mind and your body at the same time.

Rest is also so very important to allow you to truly appreciate how far you have come. When you get consistently good rest you will find that your start and end of day will be calmer and more in control. Sleep will be key to increasing your energy throughout the day and reducing overall stress. It can also help alleviate chronic pain. There are numerous apps that will help you track and guide you to improved sleep. You can start on your own by setting a consistent bed and wake time. This will create a pattern that your mind and body will begin to crave. I have a weighted blanket and eye mask. As soon as I get into bed and put on that mask, my body has been trained to turn down the noise in my head and move into a sleep state.

CHALLENGE:

Devote 10-15 minutes a day for the next 30 days to stretching, you are working toward increased mobility, clarity of thought and focused awareness of your body and how it reacts to different movements. To get the most out of this challenge it is wise to set up a location to stretch and set your Intention to stretch: "I will [Stretch] at [TIME] in [LOCATION]." That intention can be written in your journal each day over the next 30 along with any notes you have of what you observed in your physical and mental response to the stretches for that given day.

Notes

21

Fuel Your Fire

You want to be strong? You want to get fit? You want to stay fit? It all starts with the fuel you fuel your body with. Eating clean food will not only help you to reach your physical goals but it also helps your mental game so that you can achieve gains at work. A poor diet can lead to poor physical and mental health. It can increase stress and depression. It could even lead to issues with brain function and decision making.

Choose healthier food. The less processed the better. By eating a rainbow of vegetables and fruits, along with quality meats and other protein sources you can reduce inflammation, allowing your body to absorb the nutrients you need. I highly recommend adding a nutritionist and a naturopathic doctor to your list of coaches. Through their help and your execution, you will see improvements not only in your physical health but in your mental and in your successes at work.

Your heart loves you when you take care of your whole being. It is so tempting to grab a bag of chips from the vending machine when you are stressed. Just like you plan your projects at work, plan your fuel as well. Be mindful and balanced when you are snacking. Having a stash of portable non-perishable snacks in your desk, bag or car is a winning move. These could be nuts, trail mix or jerky. If you have the ability to keep your snacks cold, then leverage yogurt, cottage cheese, berries. When you pair a protein with a fat or carbohydrate you better balance blood sugar and energy levels.

These small steps add up in a big way to help with your overall health and elevate your MIGHT.

CHALLENGE:

Over the next 30 days add a new fruit or vegetable to your shopping list. Then actually eat it. You may find something new and colorful that you love. Who know if passion fruit or turnips become your new favorite.

Notes

22

Time To Compete

As you continue to level up, you will quickly realize that your physical health has a direct connection to your ability to achieve all of your other goals. In order to achieve your fitness targets, it will be critical to plan ahead. For example, if you are looking to gain muscle, hiring a fitness coach could really help. If you are struggling with nutrition, a nutritionist is key. If you are serious about your goals taking these steps can motivate you to reach them. Planning ahead translates into you building a plan with experts that will get you where you need to go. I have all sorts of coaches in my life - some are virtual, and some are in person. The ones that have had the largest impact in my life were the ones that helped me on my fitness journey. I'm not sure I could have lost 50 pounds (and kept it off) if it wasn't for those coaches that helped me to set and stay focused on my fitness goals. Set your goals. Build your plan to achieve them. Go crush them.

Do you compete? If not, it is time to start. By competing physically in races or fitness challenges, you are setting the stage to level up. Pick something you know you can have fun with. Don't take yourself too seriously. When you can smile through the journey you know you are on the right path. It allows you to stay positive. That in turn will enhance your performance.

CHALLENGE:

Sign up for a competition today. Don't wait. Sign up, Commit. Execute. You will be glad you did.

Notes

Conclusion

You have invested the time and energy into yourself by spending time learning about Might In Motion. The four pillars that now define you – **Motivation, Momentum, Mindfulness, Might** – will propel you further in your personal and professional growth. The challenges are there for you to build habits in each of these areas of your life. As you follow them you will grow. Beautifully you can revisit any one of them whenever you feel a need to reset that area of your own Might In Motion journey. Leverage these tools and embody the Might In Motion within you.

Acknowledgments

Thank you so much to my husband, Justin, who supported me in this idea to write a book.

Thank you to Dr. Danita Morales Ramos for helping me to be a better person. The skills you have taught me have been priceless!

Thank you to Alana Riley. She leant me eyes and thoughts on this book throughout the process. Your belief in me and my vision will never be forgotten.

About The Author

Marianna Kinnee is the founder of Might In Motion, LLC. She holds a Bachelor's of Science from Georgia Tech. Marianna has spent over two decades as a leader at a Global Fortune 50 company and currently leads cutting edge transportation initiatives.

Marianna has been married for over 10 years and has two daughters. She lives in Marietta, GA, where she enjoys helping with her daughter's American Heritage Girls troop, working out, gardening and reading.

Marianna's passion is building positive legacies of financial and emotional freedom. Marianna coaches like minded individuals who need help navigating their personal and professional goals to manifest them into their deserved career and life path.